EARTH**ROCKS!**
VOLCANOES

BY SARA GILBERT

CREATIVE EDUCATION • CREATIVE PAPERBACKS

Published by Creative Education and Creative Paperbacks
P.O. Box 227, Mankato, Minnesota 56002
Creative Education and Creative Paperbacks are
imprints of The Creative Company
www.thecreativecompany.us

Design and production by Chelsey Luther
Art direction by Rita Marshall
Printed in the United States of America

Photographs by Alamy (Design Pics Inc, LOOK Die Bildagentur der
Fotografen GmbH), Dreamstime (TMarchev), Getty Images (Danita
Delimont, Telusa Fotu/AFP, Jon Vidar Sigurdsson, Jim Smithson),
iStockphoto (brytta, nstanev, shirophoto, tobiasjo), Minden Pictures
(Sergey Gorshkov), National Geographic Creative (WILD WONDERS
OF EUROPE/LUNDGREN/NATUREPL.COM), Shutterstock (AvDe,
c1a1p1c1o1m1), Spoon Graphics (Chris Spooner)

Library of Congress Cataloging-in-Publication Data
Names: Gilbert, Sara.
Title: Volcanoes / Sara Gilbert.
Series: Earth Rocks!
Includes bibliographical references and index.
Summary: An elementary exploration of volcanoes, focusing on the
geological evidence that helps explain how and where they form and
spotlighting famous examples, such as Hawaii's Mauna Loa.
Identifiers: ISBN 978-1-60818-896-3 (hardcover) / ISBN 978-1-62832-
512-6 (pbk) / ISBN 978-1-56660-948-7 (eBook)

This title has been submitted for CIP processing under
LCCN 2017937622.

CCSS: RI.1.1, 2, 4, 5, 6, 7; RI.2.2, 5, 6, 7, 10; RI.3.1, 5, 7, 8; RF.1.1, 3, 4; RF.2.3, 4

First Edition HC 9 8 7 6 5 4 3 2 1
First Edition PBK 9 8 7 6 5 4 3 2 1

Pictured on cover: Tungurahua, Ecuador (top)

TABLE OF CONTENTS

SMOKE IN THE SKY

Smoke rises from the mountaintop. You hear a low rumble. You are near an active volcano. Look out—it is about to **erupt**!

VOLCANOES ERUPT!

A volcano is an opening in Earth's surface. Often, that opening is at the top of a mountain.

Ash, smoke, **lava**, and gas come out when the volcano erupts. The smoke can block the sun and make it dark.

MOUNTAINS OF MAGMA

Tectonic plates are huge slabs of rock on Earth's **crust**. Many volcanoes form along the edges of the plates.

As those plates move, they can cause **earthquakes**. They can also make way for **magma**. When magma reaches the surface, a volcano erupts.

cinder cone volcano

MOUNT BROMO

composite volcano

MOUNT FUJI

shield volcano

HALEMA'UMA'U CRATER OF KILAUEA

lava dome volcano

MOUNT ST. AUGUSTINE

EXPLODING SHAPES

There are four types of volcanoes: cinder cone, composite, shield, and lava dome. Each has a different shape. They erupt in different ways, too.

HOT ZONES

There are more than 1,500 active volcanoes on Earth. Some are underwater! More than half of the world's volcanoes are in the Ring of Fire. This is a chain of volcanoes in the Pacific Ocean.

UNDERSEA VOLCANO

MOUNT FUJI

VISITING VOLCANOES

The largest active volcano is in Hawaii. It is called Mauna Loa. From its underwater base to its top, it is taller than Mount Everest! Mount Fuji is a famous volcano in Japan. Many people try to climb it.

Some volcanoes are safe to climb. You can hike around them and have fun. But always pay attention and be careful!

ACTIVITY: VINEGAR VOLCANO

Materials

2 tablespoons baking soda

1/2 teaspoon salt

Liquid dish soap

Orange food coloring

Vinegar

Scissors

Party hat

Small glass jar

1. Cut the tip off the party hat; cut zigzags around the top.

2. In the small jar, mix the baking soda, salt, and a few drops of food coloring.

3. Add a squirt or two of liquid dish soap on top of the mixture.

4. Put the party hat (pointy end up) over the jar. Carefully pour the vinegar through the top of the hat. Watch as bubbles and gases escape through the opening. Your volcano is erupting!

GLOSSARY

crust: the outermost layer of the earth

earthquakes: sudden, violent shakings of the earth caused by the sliding of tectonic plates

erupt: for volcanoes, to become active and eject lava, smoke, gas, and ash

lava: hot liquid rock that erupts from a volcano

magma: hot liquid rock beneath the earth's crust

READ MORE

Schreiber, Anne. *Volcanoes!* Washington, D.C.: National Geographic, 2008.

Simon, Seymour. *Volcanoes*. New York: HarperCollins, 2006.

WEBSITES

Discovery Kids: Volcano Explorer

http://discoverykids.com/games/volcano-explorer/

Play fun volcano games as you learn!

National Geographic Kids: Volcano

*http://kids.nationalgeographic.com/explore/science
/volcano/#volcano-explode.jpg*

Learn interesting facts about volcanoes.

Note: Every effort has been made to ensure that any websites listed above were active at the time of publication and suitable for children. However, because of the nature of the Internet, it is impossible to guarantee that these sites will remain active indefinitely or that their contents will not be altered.

INDEX